2

DATE DUE

APR 2 4 2006			

DEMCO 128-5046

THE SOLAR SYSTEM

NEPTUNE

A MyReportLinks.com Book

GLENN SCHERER & MARTY FLETCHER

MyReportLinks.com Books

an imprint of

 Enslow Publishers, Inc.

Box 398, 40 Industrial Road
Berkeley Heights, NJ 07922
USA

MyReportLinks.com Books, an imprint of Enslow Publishers, Inc. MyReportLinks®
is a registered trademark of Enslow Publishers, Inc.

Library of Congress Cataloging-in-Publication Data

Scherer, Glenn.
    Neptune / Glenn Scherer & Marty Fletcher.
        p. cm. — (The solar system)
    Includes bibliographical references and index.
    ISBN 0-7660-5211-7
    1. Neptune (Planet)—Juvenile literature. I. Fletcher, Marty. II. Title. III. Series: Solar system (Berkeley
Heights, N.J.)

    QB691.S34 2005
    523.48'1—dc22
                                                            2004016964

Printed in the United States of America

10 9 8 7 6 5 4 3 2 1

To Our Readers:
Through the purchase of this book, you and your library gain access to the Report Links that specifically back
up this book.
The Publisher will provide access to the Report Links that back up this book and will keep these Report Links
up to date on **www.myreportlinks.com** for five years from the book's first publication date.
We have done our best to make sure all Internet addresses in this book were active and appropriate when we went
to press. However, the author and the Publisher have no control over, and assume no liability for, the material
available on those Internet sites or on other Web sites they may link to.
The usage of the MyReportLinks.com Books Web site is subject to the terms and conditions stated on the Usage
Policy Statement on **www.myreportlinks.com**.
A password may be required to access the Report Links that back up this book. The password is found on the
bottom of page 4 of this book.
Any comments or suggestions can be sent by e-mail to comments@myreportlinks.com or to the address on the
back cover.

Photo Credits: © Corel Corporation, p. 13; © Windows to the Universe, pp. 19, 27; Clipart.com, p. 37;
HubbleSite, p. 18; Johns Hopkins University Applied Physics Laboratory/Southwest Research Institute, p. 44;
Lunar and Planetary Institute, pp. 16, 22; MyReportLinks.com Books, p. 4; National Aeronautics and Space
Administration (NASA), pp. 1, 3, 9, 14, 20, 24, 25, 26, 28, 30, 32, 34, 35, 36, 38, 40, 41, 42; Photos.com,
pp. 3, 9; University of St. Andrews, pp. 11, 12.

Note: Some NASA photos were only available in a low-resolution format.

Cover Photo: National Aeronautics and Space Administration.

MyReportLinks.com Books
Great Books, Great Links, Great for Research!

The Internet sites listed on the next four pages can save you hours of research time. These Internet sites—we call them "Report Links"—are constantly changing, but we keep them up to date on our Web site.

Give it a try! Type http://www.myreportlinks.com into your browser, click on the series title, then the book title, and scroll down to the Report Links listed for this book.

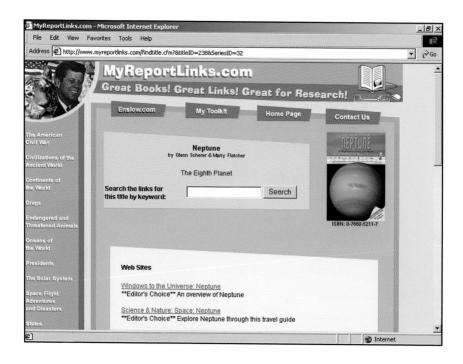

The Report Links will bring you to great source documents, photographs, and illustrations. MyReportLinks.com Books save you time, feature Report Links that are kept up to date, and make report writing easier than ever!

Please see "To Our Readers" on the copyright page for important information about this book, the MyReportLinks.com Web site, and the Report Links that back up this book.

Please enter **PNE1713** if asked for a password.

Report Links

 The Internet sites described below can be accessed at http://www.myreportlinks.com

*EDITOR'S CHOICE

▶**Windows to the Universe: Neptune**
This Web site offers a great deal of information about Neptune, including facts about the interior and surface of the planet, its atmosphere, its moons and rings, and more.

*EDITOR'S CHOICE

▶**Science & Nature: Space: Neptune**
From the BBC comes a site with basic information, videos, pictures, and links to other resources about Neptune. The site also contains links to many other sites about the solar system.

*EDITOR'S CHOICE

▶**Welcome to the Planets: Neptune**
This site from NASA's Jet Propulsion Laboratory offers images of Neptune and the other planets in the solar system. Click on each image to find a more detailed explanation of Neptune's features, moons, and rings.

*EDITOR'S CHOICE

▶**Planetary Photojournal**
Over seventy images of Neptune, its ring system, and its satellites are available through this NASA site. Every image has a full explanation and a link to a high-resolution image.

*EDITOR'S CHOICE

▶**Neptune: Eighth Planet From the Sun**
Learn about stormy Neptune and its satellites from the Planetary Society. Included are articles about past and current explorations of Neptune as well as images and links to information on other planets.

*EDITOR'S CHOICE

▶**Stardate Online: Neptune**
From the University of Texas's McDonald Observatory comes a Neptune site with basic facts and links to dozens of stories about Neptune and its satellites.

Report Links

The Internet sites described below can be accessed at http://www.myreportlinks.com

▶**Ask an Astronomer for Kids!: Neptune**

This site from the California Institute of Technology offers quick answers to kids' basic questions about Neptune. The Web site also includes images of Neptune and a diagram of Neptune's orbit.

▶**Astrogeology Research Program: Neptune**

This site from the United States Geological Survey provides information about Neptune and its moons. Names of craters and other features are provided for major moons, and images are included.

▶**Astronomy: Planets—Neptune**

This British site provides a wealth of statistics on Neptune, from the composition of its atmosphere to the orbital period of its satellites.

▶**Exploring the Planets: Neptune**

This Web site from the Smithsonian's National Air and Space Museum takes a look at the planet Neptune, its atmosphere, its moon, and its rings. Images of the planet are also included.

▶**Galileo Galilei**

From Florence's Institute and Museum of the History of Science comes a biography of Galileo Galilei, the man who observed, but did not discover, Neptune in 1612.

▶**The Hubble Project**

Learn more about the Hubble Space Telescope from this site. The Hubble and *Voyager 2* identified eleven of Neptune's moons.

▶**John Couch Adams**

A biography of John Couch Adams, one of the men who discovered Neptune, is offered at this site from the University of St. Andrews, Scotland.

▶**Mathematical Discovery of Planets**

Read about the missed opportunities, petty quarrels, and other complications that accompanied the discovery of Neptune. Along the way, learn how planets can be discovered without observing them.

Report Links

The Internet sites described below can be accessed at http://www.myreportlinks.com

▶**Mythweb—Poseidon**

The name of the planet Neptune comes from the name of the god of the sea in Roman mythology. In Greek mythology, the same god was known as Poseidon. Read about the mythological Poseidon at this site.

▶**Neptune**

This site offers animations of Neptune's orbit and rotation as well as other images of the eighth planet from the Sun.

▶**Neptune: Enigmatic Stormy Gas Ball**

This site offers a brief overview and images of Neptune. It also accepts e-mail questions from students interested in space.

▶*New Horizons*

Exploration of the solar system beyond Neptune will continue with the *New Horizons* probe, a project of the Johns Hopkins University Applied Physics Lab.

▶**Newsdesk Neptune**

Views of Neptune captured by the Hubble Space Telescope are available at this site.

▶**Nine Planets: Neptune**

This Web site provides an overview of Neptune, the eighth planet from the Sun in our solar system.

▶**Planetary Missions, Data, and Information: Neptune**

This NASA archive offers images of Neptune and its moons taken by *Voyager 2*. Also included are resources about Neptune's ring system and a further reading list.

▶**The Planet Neptune**

This comprehensive site offers a good introduction to Neptune, its moons, its rings, and its place in the solar system. Images from *Voyager 2* and Hubble are highlights.

Report Links

The Internet sites described below can be accessed at http://www.myreportlinks.com

▶**Sedna (2003 VB12)**

This site, from the codiscoverer of Sedna, describes the recent discovery of this Trans-Neptunian Object, or TNO, which is named for an Inuit goddess.

▶**The Solar System: Neptune**

This Web site from the *New York Times* provides statistics on Neptune and its moons Nereid and Triton. Articles related to the planet can also be found here.

▶**Solar System Exploration: Kuiper Belt**

The Kuiper Belt is a disk-shaped region of icy debris beyond Neptune that is more than 7.5 billion miles from the Sun. Learn more about this region from this NASA Web site.

▶**Solar System Exploration: Neptune**

From NASA comes a helpful overview of Neptune, its rings, and its satellites. Measurements are available in both English and metric notation. Images of Neptune are included.

▶**The Space Educator's Handbook: Neptune**

From the Space Educator's Handbook comes a site with basic information about Neptune that compares it to its "sister planet," Uranus. This site features detailed information on two of Neptune's satellites, Triton and Nereid.

▶**Triton: Background and Science**

Neptune's largest moon, Triton, is profiled in this site, which includes information on its icy surface and volcanic activity. Included are links to sixteen other articles about Triton.

▶**Urbain Jean Joseph Le Verrier**

Frenchman Urbain Le Verrier was first given credit for the discovery of Neptune, a feat which he now shares with John Couch Adams and Johann Galle. Learn more about Le Verrier at this British site.

▶**Voyager**

At this NASA site, read about the Voyager space probes, launched in 1977, which continue to travel to the outer reaches of the universe and beyond. In 1989, *Voyager 2* became the first spacecraft to fly by and observe Neptune.

Neptune Facts

Age
About 4.5 billion years

Diameter at Equator
30,776 miles (49,528 kilometers)

Composition
Thick atmosphere of hydrogen, helium, methane, ammonia, and water, with a dense rocky core

Average Distance From the Sun
About 2.8 billion miles (4.5 billion kilometers)

Closest Approach to Earth
About 2.7 billion miles (4.4 billion kilometers)

Orbital Period (year, in Earth years)
164.79 years

Rotational Period (day, in Earth hours)
16 hours 7 minutes

Mass
About 17 times Earth's mass

Temperature
−353°F (−214°C) at the cloud tops

Number of Moons
Thirteen, in order of distance from Neptune (closest to farthest): Naiad, Thalassa, Despina, Nereid, Galatea, Larissa, Proteus, Triton, S/2002 N1, S/2002 N2, S/2002 N3, S/2002 N4, S/2003 N1

Number of Rings
Six: Galle, Le Verrier, Lassell, Arago, Adams, and the sixth ring yet unnamed

Surface Gravity
118 percent of Earth's gravity (A person who weighs 100 pounds on Earth would weigh 110 pounds on Neptune.)

The Planet Found With Pen and Paper

On a starry night in 1781, English astronomer William Herschel gazed through his telescope and found the planet Uranus. It was the first planet in modern times to be discovered with a telescope, and its discovery caused great excitement. But with that discovery also came a great mystery.

As time passed, astronomers noticed that Uranus was drifting from its predicted orbit around the Sun. The planet's path did not follow the mathematical equations that explained how all planets are supposed to move. It was as if the gravity of some unseen object were tugging the planet out and away from the Sun.

Observers became convinced that the cause of this tug must be the gravitational pull of a huge unknown planet orbiting beyond Uranus. But where, they wondered, should they look for such a faint distant object in all the vastness of space?

▶ A Calculated Find

Some scientists thought that it might be possible to use mathematics to compare the difference between the real orbit of Uranus and its predicted orbit and pinpoint the planet beyond it. Most scientists of the day, however, thought that calculating the hidden planet's position would be impossible.

But two scholars decided to try. Unknown to each other, Englishman John Couch Adams and Frenchman Urbain Le Verrier set out to find the missing planet. The object that each man was searching for was beyond the reach of any telescope of the time. Their search was done with pen and paper.

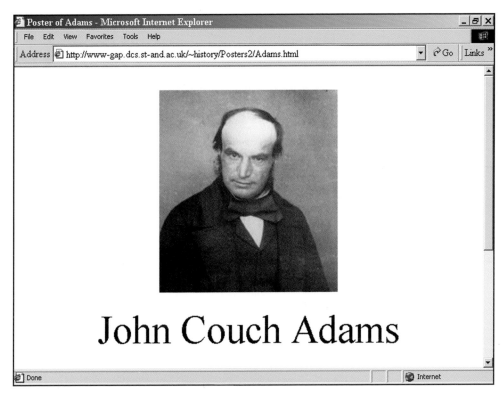

John Couch Adams

▲ Neptune was first discovered not through the lens of a telescope but through the calculations of two astronomers, working independently of one another, in different countries. One of those astronomers was John Couch Adams.

Adams was a young, shy, but brilliant mathematician and astronomer. As a boy, he amazed others by being able to perform complex calculations in his head. In 1843, while an undergraduate at Cambridge University, Adams began his determined search for the mysterious planet beyond Uranus by using what was then known about how the planets moved. Two years later, he felt sure he had calculated where the unknown planet could be found. He submitted his findings on paper to the director of the Cambridge Observatory, but unfortunately, no action was taken because most British astronomers of the time did not trust Adams's calculations.

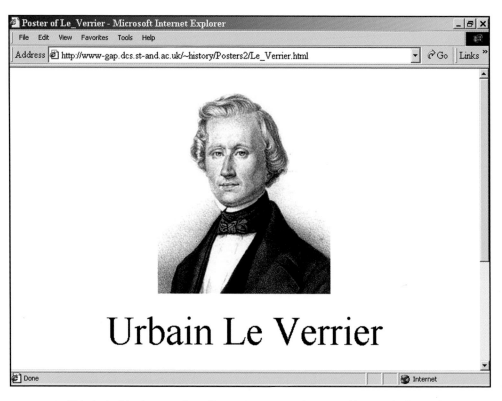

Urbain Le Verrier

▲ Urbain Le Verrier was the other astronomer who was able to calculate where the unknown planet, which we now call Neptune, could be found.

Meanwhile, in France, that country's most famous astronomer was also busy with pen and paper, trying to find the planet beyond Uranus that explained its unusual motion. Between 1845 and 1846, Urbain Le Verrier also calculated where astronomers should look to find this planet, selecting the same location that Adams had.

Le Verrier also failed to get his countrymen to make a telescopic search, so he gave his calculations to German astronomer Johann Galle, who worked at the Berlin Observatory. On the night of September 23, 1846, Galle pointed his nine-inch refracting telescope at the part of the sky where Le Verrier said the planet should be.

▲ *Neptune, the god of the sea in Roman mythology, was also the brother of the gods Jupiter and Pluto.* Neptune *was Urbain Le Verrier's choice for the name of the newly discovered planet.*

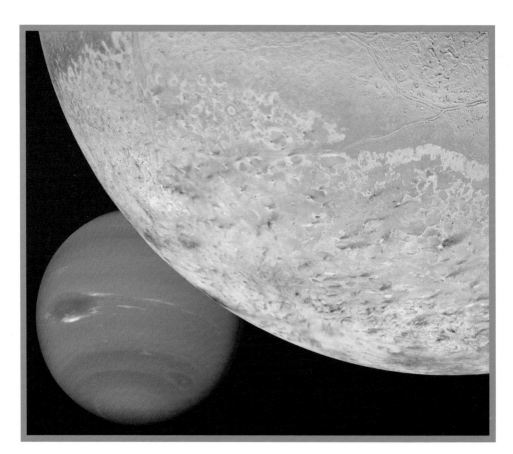

▲ *This computer-generated image combines a photograph of Neptune, the smaller blue body, and one of Triton, Neptune's largest moon. The images have been placed to capture the view one might get from a spacecraft if it were approaching Triton.*

▷ A Very Faint "Star" Is Spotted

Galle slowly called out the positions of known stars to his assistant, Heinrich d'Arrest. The assistant checked off each star on a star chart. Suddenly, Galle called out the position of a very faint "star" in the constellation of Aquarius. D'Arrest answered excitedly, "That star is not on the chart!"[1] That "star" was the previously hidden planet that Adams and Le Verrier had been seeking, and Galle found it only an hour after the telescopic search began. The next day, Galle sent a message to Le Verrier in France, saying, "The planet whose position you have pointed out *actually exists.*"[2] It was exactly where both Le Verrier and Adams had said it would be.

Naming the new planet turned out to be difficult. Galle wanted to call it Janus, after the god in Roman mythology who guarded the doors to heaven. But Le Verrier disagreed. At first he wanted to call the new planet Neptune after the Roman god of the sea, and then he decided to name the planet after himself. But the British newspapers angrily pointed out that Adams had made his calculations before Le Verrier, so the British should name the planet.

For a time, French and British newspapers attacked each other's astronomers, each claiming the new planet for their own countries. Both Adams and Le Verrier ignored these battles and instead became good friends. In the end, the name *Neptune,* Le Verrier's original choice, was chosen. That name fits the planet, with its deep-blue, oceanlike appearance.

A Great Leap Forward

The discovery of Neptune was a great step forward for science. Adams and Le Verrier had proven that mathematics could be a useful tool in astronomy and that scientists from different countries could work together successfully to make discoveries. By the twentieth century, an improved version of the math done by Adams and Le Verrier would help guide the *Voyager 2* space probe on its 2.8 billion-mile (4.5 billion-kilometer) journey to Neptune. This space probe, one of two launched in 1977 to fly by the outer planets, beamed astounding photos of Neptune's rings and moons back to Earth. With that accomplishment, astronomers learned more about the mysterious planet we call Neptune than anyone had learned in the 143 years since its discovery by Adams, Le Verrier, and Galle.

A Gas Giant in the Depths of Space

Neptune, the eighth planet from the Sun, is one of the four outer planets in the solar system. Jupiter, Saturn, and Uranus are the others. These four are known as gas giants because they have massive atmospheres made up of gases that surround small rocky cores. They are also far larger than Mercury, Venus, Earth, and Mars—the four small planets closest to the Sun. Neptune has a diameter at its equator of 30,776 miles (49,528 kilometers), making it about four times larger across than Earth. Nearly sixty Earths could fit inside the giant Neptune.

After Neptune's discovery, scientists thought that Neptune and Uranus were sister planets because they were nearly the same size

▲ Jupiter, Saturn, Uranus, and Neptune are known as gas giants because they are gigantic when compared with Earth, and they are composed mostly of gases.

and same bright blue color, and both had similar atmospheres. But those scientists could never be sure that the planets were twins because Neptune is so distant and so difficult to see. Even the very largest Earth-based telescopes could enlarge the planet to no more than a small blue dot. Neptune is nearly 2.8 billion miles (4.5 billion kilometers) from the Sun—so far away that if it were possible to drive to Neptune from the Sun in a car going at 60 miles per hour (97 kilometers per hour), it would take more than 46 million years to get there.

Cold, Dark, and Distant

Neptune is so far from the heart of the solar system that the Sun as seen from Neptune looks merely like a bright star, appearing only a little bigger in size than the head of a pin held at arm's length. Neptune receives nine hundred times less sunlight than Earth does, making Neptune a very dark place. Astronomers say that on the sunniest day on Neptune, there is only about as much light as there is on Earth a half hour after sunset.

Neptune is also very cold. The Sun is so far away that it adds almost no warmth to the planet. Temperatures in Neptune's upper clouds stay at about −353°F (−214°C). Those temperatures would be even lower if the planet did not somehow mysteriously make some of its own heat from within.

Weird Weather on Neptune

Because Neptune is so cold, scientists were sure that the planet was a dead, frozen world where nothing much happened. But in 1989, *Voyager 2* proved them wrong.

As the space probe approached the planet, its cameras sent back pictures of Neptune that showed wildly swirling clouds. Those clouds proved that instead of being a world where not much happened, Neptune has an atmosphere that is violently active—rocked by storms worse than any ever seen on Earth. Scientists have recorded fierce wind gusts on Neptune of 1,250 miles per hour

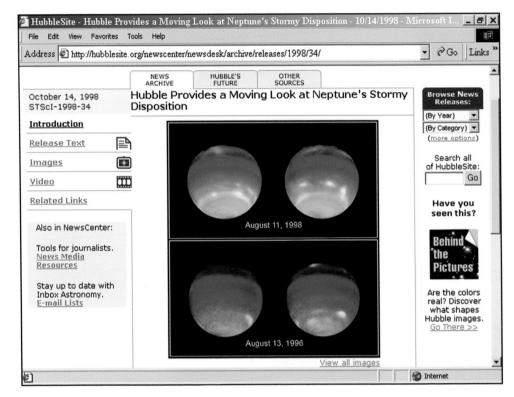

🔺 *These colorized time-lapse pictures of Neptune were taken by the Hubble Space Telescope and NASA's Infrared Telescope Facility on Mauna Kea, Hawaii. The bands show wild weather patterns on Neptune that scientists still cannot fully explain.*

(2,011 kilometers per hour). No stronger wind has been recorded in the solar system.

By comparison, the fastest wind speed ever measured on Earth was from a tornado that hit the suburbs of Oklahoma City, Oklahoma, in 1999.[1] That tornado's winds were measured at 318 miles per hour (511 kilometers per hour)—strong enough to crush buildings, rip trees from the ground, and toss three-ton cars through the air like missiles. But that tornado's winds blew with only about one fourth the speed of the fastest winds on Neptune.

As *Voyager 2* swept past the planet, its cameras recorded violent and colorful storms. It snapped pictures of streaming cloud bands and spinning spots. The biggest hurricane-like storm of all was the Great Dark Spot, a mass of twirling clouds nearly the size of Earth. Scientists guessed that such a big storm would last for a very long time, just like the famous Great Red Spot on Jupiter— a storm that has raged for more than three hundred years. (Although the storm was first spotted in the 1660s, scientists now think that it may have started long before that time.) But in 1994, only five years after *Voyager 2* left Neptune, the Hubble Space Telescope found that Neptune's Great Dark Spot had vanished without a trace.

Voyager 2 also observed other cloud features in Neptune's atmosphere. The Great Dark Spot and the Little Dark Spot (also

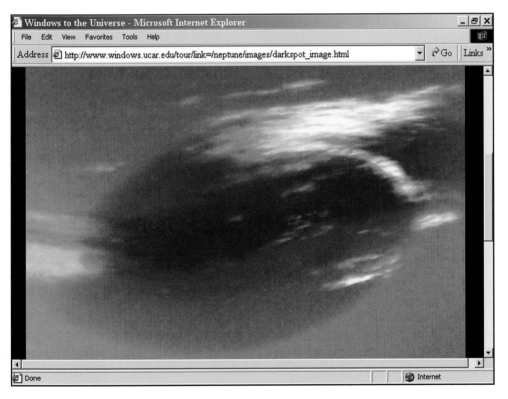

In 1989, the Voyager 2 *space probe captured this image of Neptune's Great Dark Spot, a huge mass of clouds in Neptune's southern hemisphere with incredibly strong winds. No longer visible, the Great Dark Spot is evidence that Neptune's atmosphere is changeable.*

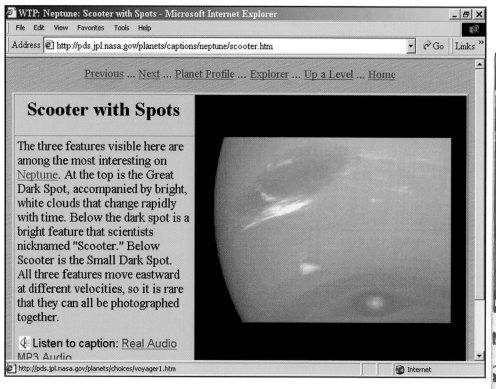

WTP: Neptune: Scooter with Spots - Microsoft Internet Explorer

File Edit View Favorites Tools Help

Address http://pds.jpl.nasa.gov/planets/captions/neptune/scooter.htm   Go   Links

Previous ... Next ... Planet Profile ... Explorer ... Up a Level ... Home

Scooter with Spots

The three features visible here are among the most interesting on Neptune. At the top is the Great Dark Spot, accompanied by bright, white clouds that change rapidly with time. Below the dark spot is a bright feature that scientists nicknamed "Scooter." Below Scooter is the Small Dark Spot. All three features move eastward at different velocities, so it is rare that they can all be photographed together.

Listen to caption: Real Audio
MP3 Audio

http://pds.jpl.nasa.gov/planets/choices/voyager1.htm   Internet

▲ *Neptune's cloud feature nicknamed Scooter is in the middle of this photograph, flanked by the Great Dark Spot, above, and the Little Dark Spot, below. Scientists chose the name Scooter because of the speed at which this cloud system sped around the planet.*

nicknamed the Wizard's Eye) seemed to race each other around the planet. Another cloud feature was named Scooter because it sped around Neptune faster than any other cloud system. By 1994, both the Little Dark Spot and the Scooter had also disappeared.[2]

Scientists have so far been unable to figure out why a planet as cold as Neptune has such violent weather. On Earth, much of our weather is driven by the power of the Sun, which warms the air and causes winds to blow and storms to happen. But the Sun's warming power is too weak to cause similar storms on Neptune. The answer might be that Neptune makes its own heat from somewhere inside the planet. Like the other gas giants, it actually gives off more heat energy than it gets from the Sun—almost three times more. Scientists are not sure why or how this happens, but they think that each giant planet is still collapsing, or compressing under its own gravity. This compression produces heat that escapes outward. It seems possible, then, that this escaping heat is the energy that drives Neptune's violent storms and winds.

Inside the Atmosphere and Into the Depths of Neptune

The only part of Neptune that is clearly visible to Earth-based telescopes and *Voyager 2* has been the top layer of its dense, swirling clouds. This atmosphere is made up of a mixture of hydrogen, helium, water, ammonia, and methane. Frozen crystals of methane whirling high in Neptune's atmosphere give Neptune its stunning blue color. (Uranus is a similar color for the same reason.) In Earth's atmosphere, methane is a gas, but temperatures are so cold on Neptune that methane can freeze solid.

Another question that continues to fascinate scientists is what lies hidden below the cloud tops of Neptune. Despite years of telescopic observations and thousands of measurements taken by *Voyager 2,* scientists can still only guess at the answer. Most think that a solid, rocky core lies at the heart of the planet. Some think that an ocean of liquid hydrogen might cover that rocky core, and on top of that may be an ocean of water. But this water ocean would be nothing like the oceans on Earth. It would lie 3,000 miles (4,828 kilometers) beneath the atmosphere and would be under intense pressure from the weight of air pressing down on it. That pressure would be 200,000 times greater than the atmospheric pressure on Earth.

If such a super-squeezed water ocean exists on Neptune, its water molecules, rubbing on each other, would have created electricity and magnetism. This theory might explain the fierce magnetic field that surrounds the planet. *Voyager 2* detected this powerful magnetic field when it was still far from Neptune.

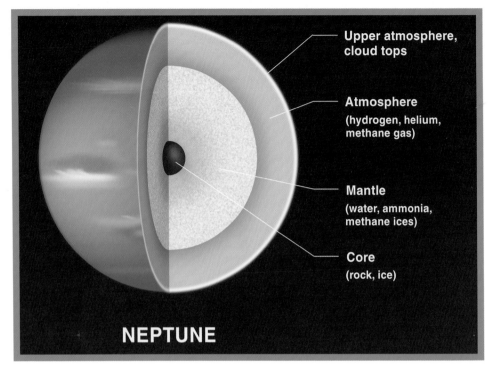

NEPTUNE

⚠ *This drawing represents the best theories that scientists have of what Neptune is made of, since all they have seen is its top layer of clouds.*

Neptune's magnetic field is more than two times stronger than Earth's magnetic field.

Unlike Earth's magnetic field, which is generated from the center, Neptune's magnetic field is way off center. The heart of Neptune's magnetic field is 8,500 miles (13,679 kilometers) from the middle of the planet. That puts it just over halfway between the planet's center and cloud tops—exactly where scientists think the super-squeezed, electrically-conductive water ocean would be located.

The magnetic field of Neptune is also tipped 47 degrees away from the axis around which the planet spins. Why Neptune's magnetic axis is tipped so steeply away from its rotational axis and offset so far from its center is still a mystery to astronomers.

Chapter 3 ▶

A Year and a Day on Neptune

Neptune is a mind-boggling distance away from the Sun. It orbits an average of 2.8 billion miles (4.5 billion kilometers) from the center of the solar system. That means that its orbit is immense, covering many billions of miles, and that its year and seasons are extremely long compared to those on Earth.

▷ Neptune's Year

Even though Neptune travels around the Sun at an average speed of more than 12,000 miles per hour (19,312 kilometers per hour), it still takes Neptune 164.79 Earth years to complete one full orbit. That means that a year on Neptune lasts more than twice the length of an average human life. In fact, the planet has yet to complete a full orbit since its discovery. It will be 2011 before Neptune will be seen again at the same place in its orbit that Johann Galle first saw it in 1846.

Another unusual fact about Neptune's orbit is that for about twenty years during each revolution of Pluto, the outermost planet, Neptune is actually farther from the Sun than Pluto is. That is because Pluto's oddly shaped orbit sometimes cuts inside Neptune's orbit. The last time this happened was between 1979 and 1999.

▷ The Seasons on Neptune

Unlike Earth, where seasons last for three months, on Neptune each season lasts more than forty years. Seasons are caused by a planet's tilt as it travels around the Sun. Earth's axis is tipped at a 23.5-degree angle from vertical. Neptune spins with a tilt of about 29 degrees. This tipping of the planet causes the northern

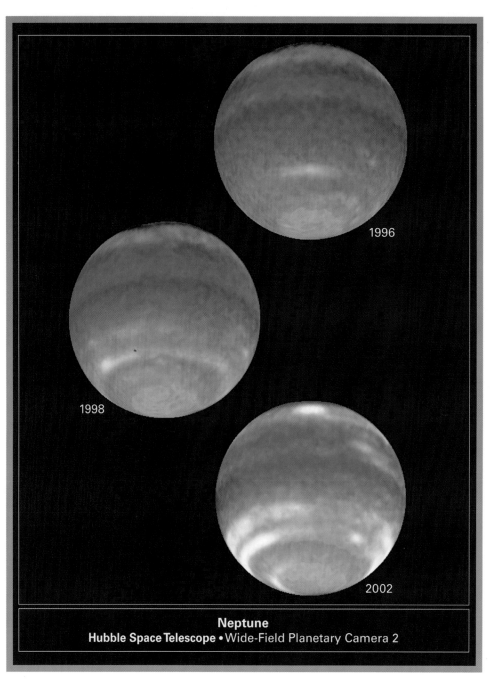

Neptune
Hubble Space Telescope • Wide-Field Planetary Camera 2

▲ Observations by the Hubble Space Telescope over time have shown an increase in the brightness of Neptune's southern hemisphere. Scientists believe that this increased brightness is a sign of seasonal change.

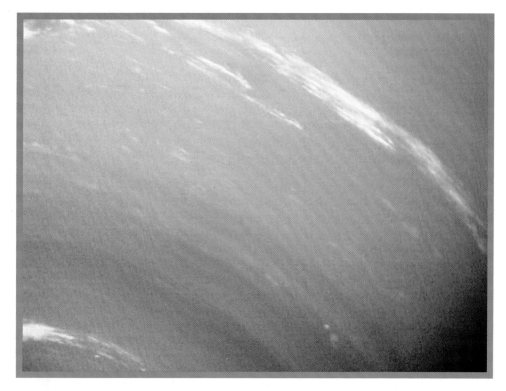

Voyager 2's wide-angle camera took this image of Neptune when the space probe was 370,000 miles (590,000 kilometers) from the planet. The image has been processed to show Neptune's cloud structure.

and southern parts of the planet, known as hemispheres, to have opposite seasons.

Between 1996 and 2002, the Hubble Space Telescope was actually able to see the coming of spring to Neptune's southern hemisphere. As astronomers watched Neptune over that six-year period, they saw the bands of clouds in the sky above the southern half of the planet get brighter and wider.[1] Similar increases in cloud cover happen on Earth as spring begins.

Neptune's Very Short Day

For many years, astronomers were unsure exactly how long a day was on Neptune. This uncertainty existed because they could not

▲ *The* Voyager 2 *spacecraft was the first to capture images of the eighth planet from the Sun. This Voyager image highlights Neptune's blue color, caused by the methane in its atmosphere.*

see the rocky surface of Neptune and also because clouds rotate at different speeds than the solid, rocky part of the planet. Without a solid point with which to mark the planet's daily spin, scientists could only guess at a day's length.

Voyager 2's arrival at the planet allowed its instruments to penetrate far below the cloud tops. The space probe discovered that Neptune, like the other gas giants, rotates very fast for such a big planet. It turns on its axis once every sixteen hours seven minutes—more than seven hours faster than the twenty-four hours it takes Earth to rotate on its axis. Neptune's spin is so fast that it has even forced the planet to bulge slightly at its equator and to be flattened at its poles, also like the other gas giants.

The Rings and Moons of Neptune

For 143 years following Neptune's discovery, scientists knew very little about the moons that orbited Neptune. They also wondered whether the planet had a complete ring system. A ring system is a band of small objects, usually dust, ice, and rocky material, that revolves around a planet.

Gerard Kuiper - Microsoft Internet Explorer

File Edit View Favorites Tools Help

Address http://www.windows.ucar.edu/tour/link=/people/today/kuiper.html Go Links

Gerard Kuiper

Gerard Kuiper was an American astronomer who lived between 1905-1973. He is considered the father of modern planetary science for his brilliant study of our solar system.

Kuiper developed new techniques of looking at the sky, and discovered a moon of Neptune and Uranus. He also found that Titan had an atmosphere similar to our own.

Kuiper suggested that there was a belt of comet-like debris at the edge of our solar system, a theory that was proven true 20 years after his death.

Portrait of Gerard Kuiper
Photograph courtesy of University of Arizona, Deparment of Planetary Sciences

Done Internet

▲ *Gerard P. Kuiper, considered the father of modern planetary science, discovered Nereid, the second of Neptune's moons to be observed, in 1949.*

On October 10, 1846, just seventeen days after Neptune was discovered by Johann Galle, its largest moon was discovered by William Lassell, an English brewer and amateur astronomer. The moon was named Triton after Poseidon's or Neptune's son in mythology. A second moon was not spotted until 1949 when American astronomer Gerard P. Kuiper first observed the moon Nereid. That small satellite was named for the sea nymphs who swam with and served Neptune, god of the sea.

In 1981, astronomers made a most astounding discovery. They were watching Neptune through their Earthbound telescopes as the planet passed in front of a star. Just before this event, called an occultation, began, the star seemed to flicker out.

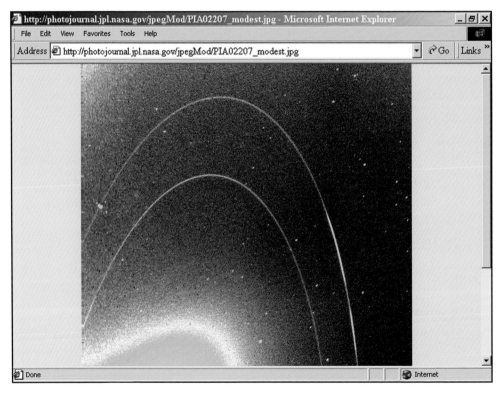

http://photojournal.jpl.nasa.gov/jpegMod/PIA02207_modest.jpg - Microsoft Internet Explorer

File   Edit   View   Favorites   Tools   Help

Address http://photojournal.jpl.nasa.gov/jpegMod/PIA02207_modest.jpg   Go   Links

Done   Internet

▲ This Voyager 2 image was the first to show Neptune's rings clearly. The two main rings are 33,000 miles (53,00 kilometers) and 39,000 miles (63,000 kilometers) from the planet.

Scientists guessed that this flicker was caused by the star's light being blocked by some object orbiting Neptune.

That object, they guessed, either had to be an undiscovered moon or a ring like the one found around Saturn. Although scientists thought that the object was a ring, *Voyager 2* showed it to be a tiny moon, later named Larissa. Then in 1983, Neptune occulted, or passed in front of, another star, and scientists were watching. Again they saw the star wink out just before Neptune passed in front of it. After this second occultation, scientists became very sure that what they were seeing was a planetary ring system rather than a tiny moon blocking the star.

But a mystery remained. When these occultations of Neptune occurred, there was always a flicker just *before* the planet passed in front of the star, never *after*. It made them wonder, if there was a complete ring around Neptune, why was starlight only blocked on one side of the planet? Any star hidden by the ring should have been hidden on both sides of the planet during an occultation. They guessed that Neptune might be the only planet in the solar system to have a partial ring circling it.

Astronomers continued trying to figure out the mystery of Neptune's ring. But they had to wait until 1989 for an answer when *Voyager 2* flew within 3,050 miles (4,908 kilometers) of the planet—the closest approach to any planet by either *Voyager 1* or *2*.

The Clumpy Rings of Neptune

As *Voyager 2* sped past Neptune, its cameras snapped away. But scientists still worried that the ring system, if it existed at all, might be too faint to be seen. One scientist commented that Neptune receives so little sunlight that its ring system would have about "half the reflectivity of soot against a black background."[1]

But *Voyager* did spot a ring system. After the craft flew past the planet, it was able to look back and see the rings backed by the Sun. What the spacecraft saw was not a partial ring system

▲ *About 3 million miles (4.8 million kilometers) from Neptune,* Voyager 2 *took this dramatic picture of the crescents of Neptune and its largest moon, Triton.*

around the planet, but four complete rings. Astronomers later realized these were actually six rings.

Five of the rings were named for the astronomers who discovered and studied Neptune. They were named for Le Verrier and Adams (who first calculated the planet's position), Galle (who first identified it through a telescope), Lassell (who discovered its largest moon), and Arago (Le Verrier's teacher, who encouraged him to study the wobbles of Uranus's orbit, which led to Neptune's discovery). One very faint ring has yet to be named.

Though *Voyager 2* solved the mystery of whether Neptune had rings, it also uncovered a new mystery. While all six rings were complete, particles within the outermost ring, the Adams ring, were not exactly evenly spread out along the ring. Some parts of this ring have just a few particles while other sections have bunched-up particles, like cars in bumper-to-bumper traffic.

Some scientists thought that these clumpy segments, called arcs, looked "a little like sausages on a string."[2]

This clumping in the outer ring explained why Earth-based astronomers had thought the rings were partial. With their telescopes, they could see only the fatter "sausage" part of the outer ring hiding the occulted stars but not the thin "stringy" sections. But what causes this clumping? And why are parts of this ring twisted like strands of rope? Scientists continue to hunt for answers, but most agree that the clumping and twisting are caused by gravity acting on the Adams ring's particles and the moon Galatea, which orbits just inside the outer ring.

The Moons of Neptune

The *Voyager 2* flyby in 1989 and observations by the Hubble Space Telescope in 2002 and 2003 identified eleven previously unknown moons orbiting Neptune. That brought the total to thirteen. Some tiny satellites were found as recently as 2003. Neptune's moons, from largest to smallest, are Triton, Proteus, Nereid, Larissa, Galatea, Despina, Thalassa, Naiad, S/2002 N4, S/2002 N1, S/2002 N2, S/2002 N3, and S/2003 N1. They range in size from 1,681 miles (2,705 kilometers) in diameter to less than 33 miles (54 kilometers) across.

Most of the moons are rocky balls covered by craters and ice. The smallest ones are irregularly shaped. Most of the moons have been named after characters in Greek and Roman mythology, like Proteus (Neptune's second largest moon) and Nereid (its third largest). The five small moons that were discovered most recently have so far been assigned numbers rather than names.

A Close Look at Triton

Neptune's largest moon, Triton, was the last object that *Voyager 2* flew by before heading out of the solar system and into deep interstellar space. Unknowingly, *Voyager*'s mission planners had saved the very best for last. Triton, it turns out, a place of many

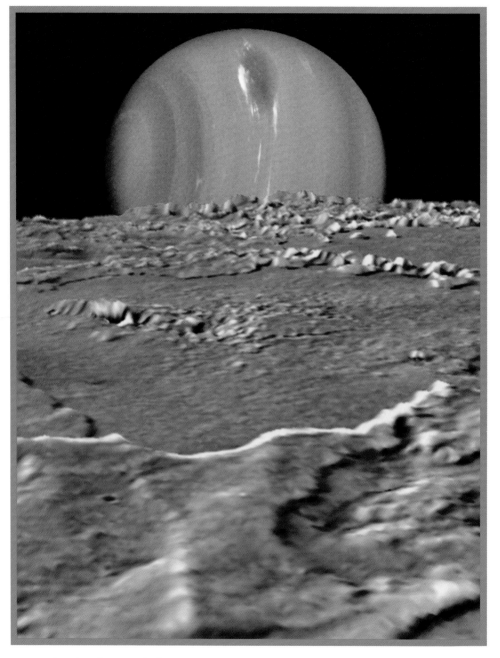

▲ This photograph showing Neptune on Triton's horizon was made by combining separate views of the planet and moon. In this image of Neptune, its south pole is to the left. Because of Triton's motion relative to Neptune, Neptune appears to move sideways rather than rising or setting.

spectacular wonders, is like no planet or moon found anywhere else in the solar system.

First of all, Triton is the only large moon in the solar system to revolve around its planet backward. All of the other large moons travel in the same direction as their mother planet's spin, but Triton travels in the opposite direction of Neptune's rotation. It does this, scientists believe, because Triton was not originally one of Neptune's moons but was captured later by the planet's gravity.

Triton is one of only three moons in the solar system to have an atmosphere, although it is a very thin one made up mostly of nitrogen and methane. The other moons with atmospheres are Titan, which orbits Saturn, and Io, which orbits Jupiter.

Cold and White as Snow

Triton is also the coldest moon in the solar system and one of the most reflective. Much of its surface is covered in mirror-bright frozen water that is as hard as granite. It is also covered in drifting methane and nitrogen "snows." The famous astronomer Carl Sagan jokingly likened the surface of Triton to a winter paradise: "In some places the surface is as bright and white as freshly fallen Antarctic snows (and may offer a skiing experience unrivaled in all the Solar System)."[3] Because Triton reflects so much light and heat away from its surface, its temperatures fall to −391°F (−235°C). And because it is so cold, scientists guessed that Triton would be a dead, inactive world. Instead, this big moon shows signs of being among the most active planetary satellites ever explored.

When seen by *Voyager 2*, the surface of Triton revealed remarkable features. They found that fractures as large as 600 miles (965 kilometers) long and 20 miles (32 kilometers) wide crisscrossed the moon. Scientists believe that these cracks in the moon's surface were created shortly after Neptune captured Triton. That capture caused such a geologic strain that Triton's surface melted. Then, as it orbited Neptune, the new moon gradually refroze from the outside in. After the surface hardened,

This photograph of the surface of Triton was taken through colored filters that highlight the moon's features, including craters and fractures.

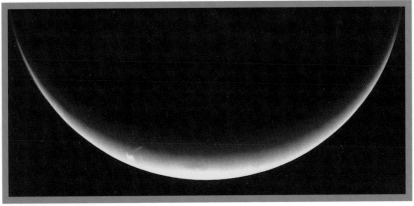

▲ *The final image of Neptune taken by* Voyager 2 *as it sped away from the planet shows Neptune's south pole.*

liquid water underground turned to ice, expanded, and cracked the refrozen outer skin. This cracking created the fractures that *Voyager* photographed.

There is also evidence of floods on Triton. Great flat basins appear to be ancient craters that have been filled up by some kind of material erupting from inside the moon.

In 1989, Laurence Soderblom, a planetary geologist from Arizona, and his coworker, Tammy Becker, made an astounding discovery about Triton. A month after the *Voyager* flyby, they were examining several pictures of Triton taken from different angles. When they matched up the photos, they saw that the terrain had changed during the brief hours of the *Voyager* flyby. What they saw were five dark clouds rising from the moon's surface. Soderblom and Becker had discovered nitrogen geysers on Triton.

These geysers shoot 5 miles (8 kilometers) into the sky. Astronomers believe the eruptions are caused by a spring thaw on Triton. As the Sun shines faintly overhead through the clear water and nitrogen ice at Triton's surface, materials underground melt and expand. Pressure builds up, until, like a pressure cooker, the lid blows off. These violent eruptions send plumes of nitrogen and other material shooting into the sky.

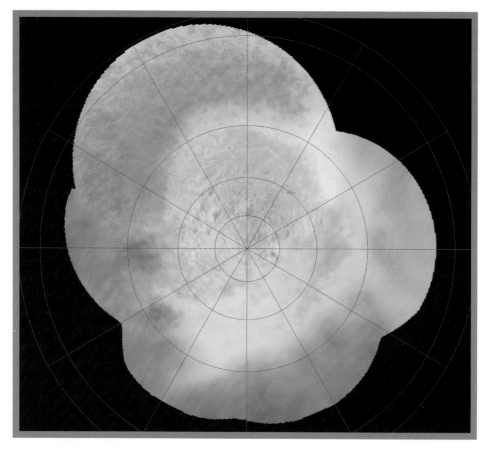

▲ The south pole of Triton is projected in this image taken by Voyager 2. Scientists think that the bright fringe of the polar cap is made of nitrogen frost or snow.

"Make no mistake about it," said *Voyager* scientist Brad Smith, referring to the geysers erupting. "These events are violent. You wouldn't want to stick your face into one of those geyser vents when it was about to go off."[4]

Triton is a world that scientists are eager to learn more about. Many now think that it is not a moon at all but an icy body like Pluto. Triton's wonders and mysteries are likely to fascinate researchers for centuries to come.

Chapter 5 ▶

Neptune Explored

If the famous early astronomer Galileo Galilei had been a little more persistent, he might have discovered Neptune almost two and a half centuries before Adams, Le Verrier, and Galle.

On the evening of December 28, 1612, Galileo observed Jupiter and its four biggest moons through his small handmade telescope. A month later, he again turned his telescope toward Jupiter. That was when he drew a small map, noting not only the positions of the planet and its moons but also a mysterious object. Galileo drew a dotted line to a "fixed star" that he believed had moved between the times of his two observations. According to scientists, that star was Neptune. Unfortunately, Galileo did not follow up on his observations, so more than 225 years would pass before Neptune was discovered.

In 1612, Galileo saw what he believed was a "fixed star" beyond Jupiter. Astronomers today believe what he actually saw was Neptune.

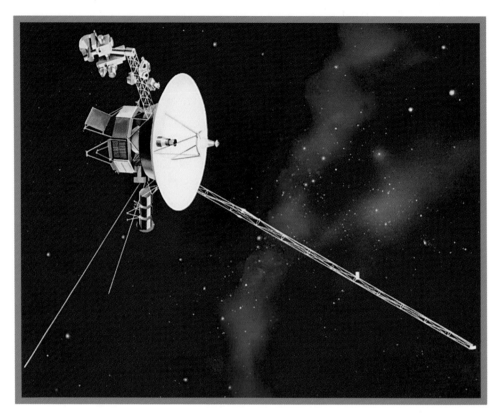

⏶ *The Voyager space probes have exceeded their original missions many times over. It is thanks to* Voyager 2 *that we now know as much as we do about Neptune.*

▷ Voyager: A Grand Tour of the Outer Solar System

Neptune, the pale blue dot that Johann Galle first saw through his telescope in 1846, remained largely a mystery until well into the twentieth century. In 1965, astronomer Mark Littman got a fascinating idea. He noticed a planetary alignment that would take place during the next two decades. In the 1970s and 1980s, Jupiter, Saturn, Neptune, and Uranus would be lined up on the same side of the Sun, allowing for a "grand tour" by an unmanned spacecraft. He believed that it might be possible to launch a robotic space probe from Earth to Jupiter and allow it to be caught in Jupiter's field of gravity and then shot on to Saturn. Using that same sling-shot effect, the probe could be flung out to Uranus, then Neptune. "I could see immediately that a single spacecraft could explore all four giant outer planets by using each planet in succession to modify the spacecraft's trajectory [path] as necessary to rendezvous with [meet up with] the next planet in the series," wrote Littman.[1]

No spacecraft had been built in 1965 that could make such a complex and difficult journey, but Littman's theory led to the construction of *Voyagers 1* and *2* in the mid-1970s. By the summer of 1977, the twin spacecraft *Voyager 1* and *Voyager 2* were successfully launched in separate months by NASA from Cape Canaveral, Florida. One of the greatest adventures in space had begun.

The original mission of the Voyager probes was to study Jupiter, Saturn, and their rings and moons, so the craft were built to last for only five years.[2] But they accomplished that mission so well that Voyager's scientists at the Jet Propulsion Laboratory, managed for NASA by the California Institute of Technology, in Pasadena, California, were not able to resist extending the mission. They even used remote-control programming to allow the Voyagers to do more while in space than they had been equipped to do at the time of launch. Although launched later, *Voyager 1* flew by Jupiter and Saturn first, followed by *Voyager 2*. But it remained for *Voyager 2* to travel farther, to Uranus and Neptune.

▶ The Farthest Target

For that mission to succeed, *Voyager 2* needed a great deal of luck—and the most careful planning possible. On its long voyage across the solar system, the space probe might be damaged by the extreme cold or hit by micrometeors, very small particles in space. Even a tiny navigational error could cause *Voyager 2* to miss its farthest target, the planet Neptune.

But *Voyager 2* was not damaged in flight, and it hit its target perfectly. After traveling for twelve years and more than 2.8 billion

In this false-color image of Neptune, areas in red represent a semitransparent haze from gases that cover the planet.

miles (4.5 billion kilometers) through the depths of space, *Voyager 2* flew within 3,050 miles (4,908 kilometers) of Neptune on August 25, 1989. The craft soared above the blue clouds and fierce swirling storms, snapping thousands of photos. Rocketing outward at 61,000 miles per hour (98,170 kilometers per hour), *Voyager 2* passed near Triton and then sped on toward the edge of the solar system.

On its grand tour, *Voyager 2* became the first spacecraft to explore four planets in a single flight. It visited fifty-six moons. It explored twenty-five worlds that had never before been visited by an Earth probe, and it discovered sixteen new worlds, each with its own amazing and startling terrain and each with a story to tell.

Neptune and Triton were the last ports of call for *Voyager 2* before it sailed away out of the solar system. But the mission continues: The twin probes are now on an amazing trip into a part of space beyond the solar system. They continue to send back signals to Earth as they journey to a place where no human-made object has ever gone before.

"The real heroes are the engineers at JPL [the Jet Propulsion Laboratory]," said scientist Scott Tremaine, talking about the people responsible for the Voyager mission. They "built the wonderful spacecraft that have lasted so long and performed so well."[3]

▷ Neptune, Pluto, Sedna, and Beyond . . .

By learning about Neptune, astronomers and other scientists have also been able to learn a great deal more than they ever knew about the outer edge of the solar system. They now know that Neptune's size and its location are the reasons that its gravity controls many objects beyond it in a region of space called the Kuiper Belt. Often referred to as the "final frontier" of our solar system, the Kuiper Belt is named for the renowned American astronomer Gerard P. Kuiper who suggested that an area of icy debris existed at the edge of the solar system.

Scientists have also found more than a thousand tiny planetoids (small planetlike bodies in space) called Trans-Neptunian Objects, or TNOs, beyond Neptune. They think that Neptune's gravity stabilizes the strange orbit that Pluto and its moon Charon share. And they also believe that Neptune's gravity affects the orbit of Halley's Comet, trapping this famous celestial body of ice and dust in a long 76-year path that passes around the Sun at one end

▲ *This painting is an artist's view of what Sedna might look like.*

Sedna
800-1100 miles
in diameter

Quaoar
(800 miles)

Pluto
(1400 miles)

Moon
(2100 miles)

Earth
(8000 miles)

A new planetoid named Sedna, even farther from Earth than Neptune is, was discovered in March 2004. This picture shows Sedna in relation to other bodies in the solar system, including Earth and its Moon, Pluto, and Quaoar, a planetoid beyond Pluto.

and turns around near Neptune's orbit at the other. The comet is expected to be seen again from Earth in 2062.

There are no plans to send new space probes to Neptune, although there is still much to learn about its cloud-capped stormy atmosphere, its hidden rocky core, and its unique rings. Planetary geologists are also eager to learn more about Triton, Neptune's largest moon and home to one of the strangest landscapes in the solar system.

The New Horizons spacecraft is part of a future mission to investigate the Kuiper Belt, a mysterious world beyond Neptune. This artist's impression shows what it might look like when that craft encounters a Kuiper Belt Object.

Beyond Neptune lies the Kuiper Belt, made up of icy bodies. In this artist's drawing, two Kuiper Belt Objects orbiting each other at the edge of our solar system are illuminated by the distant Sun, the tiny dot in the upper left corner of the picture.

But even without new space missions, there are astounding discoveries that continue to be made at the edge of the solar system. In March 2004, astronomers announced that they had found a new planetoid, a TNO, orbiting far beyond Neptune and Pluto. They named it Sedna, after the Inuit goddess of the sea. Sedna, an icy body like Triton and Pluto, is a desolate world about three quarters the size of Pluto, and it travels through eternal darkness. At its greatest distance from the Sun, Sedna's orbit lies 84 billion miles (135 billion kilometers) from the center of the solar system. That is thirty times farther away than Neptune.

"There's absolutely nothing else like it known in the solar system," said Michael Brown, whose team at the California Institute of Technology found the planetoid.[4] The discovery of Sedna reminds Earthbound humans of the amazing surprises that await us in the outer reaches of space—at Neptune, Triton, and beyond.

Glossary

fracture—Crack or fault in a rocky surface.

gas giants—The four large planets, Jupiter, Saturn, Uranus, and Neptune, at the outer edge of the solar system.

geyser—A spring that bursts above ground with water or steam.

interstellar space—The space between stars.

Kuiper Belt—A region of icy debris that exists beyond Neptune, at the edge of the solar system; named for Gerard Kuiper, considered the father of modern planetary science.

magnetic field—A region where magnetic forces can be detected.

methane—A gas that exists in frozen form on Neptune, giving the planet its blue color.

micrometeors—Small pebblelike objects in space.

occultation—The blockage of light from one celestial body by another; a planet can occult, or block, the light from a distant star.

planetary geologist—A scientist who studies the composition of a planet's solid matter.

planetoid—A small celestial body that resembles a planet.

ring system—A band of dust, ice, and/or rocks that revolves around a body in space.

Chapter 1. The Planet Found With Pen and Paper

1. Mark Littman, *Planets Beyond* (New York: Wiley Science Editions, 1990), p. 49.

2. Ibid.

Chapter 2. A Gas Giant in the Depths of Space

1. BBC News, "U.S. Tornado Breaks Records, " May 13, 1999, <http://news.bbc.co.uk/1/hi/sci/tech/342507.stm> (October 20, 2004).

2. William A. Gutsche, *1001 Things Everyone Should Know About the Universe* (New York: Doubleday, 1998), pp. 134–135.

Chapter 3. A Year and a Day on Neptune

1. Space Today, "It's Springtime on Planet Neptune," n.d., <http://www.spacetoday.org/SolSys/Neptune/NeptuneSpringtime.html> (October 20, 2004).

Chapter 4. The Rings and Moons of Neptune

1. Mark Littman, *Planets Beyond* (New York: Wiley Science Editions, 1990), p. 227.

2. Ibid.

3. Carl Sagan, *Pale Blue Dot* (New York: Random House, 1994), p. 139.

4. Littman, p. 248.

Chapter 5. Neptune Explored

1. Mark Littman, *Planets Beyond* (New York: Wiley Science Editions, 1990), p. 97.

2. NASA Jet Propulsion Laboratory, California Institute of Technology, *Voyager: The Interstellar Mission,* "Planetary Voyage," March 23, 2004, <http://voyager.jpl.nasa.gov/science/planetary.html> (October 20, 2004).

3. Littman, p. 143.

4. NASA, *NASA News,* Press release, "Most Distant Object in Solar System Discovered," March 14, 2004, <http://www.nasa.gov/home/hqnews/2004/mar/HQ_04091_sedna_discovered.html> (October 20, 2004).

Asimov, Isaac, with revisions and updating by Richard Hantula. *Neptune*. Milwaukee: Gareth Stevens Publishing, 2002.

Caprara, Giovanni, ed. *The Solar System: A Firefly Guide*. Toronto: Firefly Books, 2003.

Chartrand, Mark R. *National Audubon Society Field Guide to the Night Sky*. New York: Alfred A. Knopf, 2000.

Cole, Michael D. *Neptune: The Eighth Planet*. Berkeley Heights, N.J.: Enslow Publishers, Inc., 2002.

Kerrod, Robin. *The Far Planets*. Austin, Tex.: Raintree Steck-Vaughn, 2002.

Miller, Ron. *Extrasolar Planets*. Brookfield, Conn.: Twenty-First Century Books, 2002.

————. *Uranus and Neptune*. Brookfield, Conn.: Twenty-First Century Books, 2003.

Spangenburg, Ray, and Kit Moser. *A Look at Moons*. New York: Franklin Watts, 2000.

Standage, Tom. *The Neptune File: A Story of Astronomical Rivalry and the Pioneers of Planet Hunting*. New York: Berkley Books, 2001.

Stefoff, Rebecca. *Neptune*. New York: Benchmark Books, 2002.

Tabak, John. *A Look at Neptune*. New York: Franklin Watts, 2003.

Tobias, Russell R. *USA in Space*. Pasadena, Calif.: Salem Press, 2001.